The
Portal

ENTER INTO A NEW LIFE
FILLED WITH PURPOSE,
PEACE AND HOPE

Garth and Mary Jestley

WITH FOREWORD BY PAUL HENDERSON

THE PORTAL: ENTER INTO A NEW LIFE FILLED WITH PURPOSE, PEACE AND HOPE

Softcover ISBN: 978-1-4866-2773-8
Hardcover ISBN: 978-1-4866-2775-2
eBook ISBN: 978-1-4866-2774-5

Word Alive Press
119 De Baets Street Winnipeg, MB R2J 3R9
www.wordalivepress.ca

WORD ALIVE
—P R E S S—

Cataloguing in Publication information can be obtained from Library and Archives Canada.

I am the door. If anyone enters
by me, he will be saved and
will go in and out and find
pasture. The thief comes only
to steal and kill and destroy. I
came that they may have life
and have it abundantly.[1]

—Jesus

[1] John 10:9–10, ESV.

CONTENTS

CONTENTS

FOREWORD

IN MY FORMER life, I fulfilled my boyhood dream of becoming a professional hockey player. I was thoroughly enjoying my career in the National Hockey League and couldn't imagine doing anything else. To top it off, I was catapulted into the national spotlight when I scored the winning goal in the 1972 Summit Series between Canada and the former Soviet Union. That winning goal became so famous that the Canadian Press named it the "Sports Moment of the Century."

Despite the many accolades and national recognition, I became increasingly restless and began questioning whether there was any real meaning or purpose to life. Finally, at the age of thirty-two, I invited Jesus to become my Lord and Savior. It is no exaggeration to say that everything changed from that moment! And not long afterward, my wife Eleanor did the same. We have now spent decades living out our joint calling as followers of Jesus.

Eleanor and I have known Garth and Mary Jestley, the co-authors of this book, for many years and can attest to their personal passion for following Jesus. Along the way, they, like us, have discovered that Jesus is the doorway to a life of purpose, fulfillment, peace, and hope. Assuming you want this too, we encourage you to read on!

—Paul Henderson, CM, OOnt

INTRODUCTION

WHILE IN MY mid-thirties, I found myself increasingly dissatisfied with my career. On the outside, I had all the trappings of success. On the inside, I was empty. As a result, I began wondering about the purpose of my life, particularly in light of all the stress and drivenness I was experiencing.

Then, in a single moment—and with a big shoutout to Mary, my wife and co-author—I discovered my purpose!

This book was born out of Mary's and my desire to share that discovery with anyone else plagued by the same disquieting questions that motivated my search for fulfillment. Perhaps you too have asked yourself some or all of the following big questions.

- Does my life have purpose beyond achieving personal goals and receiving recognition for my performance?
- Am I fulfilled in my personal and professional life?
- Am I experiencing inner peace even, or particularly, in the midst of big challenges?
- Do I have any hope for my future?

As discussed hereafter, we can answer all four of these questions with a resounding yes!

My 180-degree turnabout followed a dramatic encounter with Jesus Christ after a big corporate promotion caused me to question whether there was more to life than professional success.

Mary's followed an equally dramatic encounter with Jesus after a diligent search for truth.

Before you discount the message of this book as religious musings lacking relevance to your own personal and professional life, we encourage you to consider the fact that we didn't become followers of Jesus because of major life reversals such as illness, financial woes, or business problems. Quite the contrary! As previously mentioned, my professional life was progressing well and our family life was happy.

Moreover, rather than change vocation, I continued in business, ultimately serving as CEO of a successful international investment management firm. And notwithstanding many professional and personal challenges over the years, Mary and I both found purpose and experienced fulfillment, peace, and hope as we leaned into our newfound relationship with Jesus.

Finally, we are well-read regarding the various objections to the truth of the Christian worldview, including the trustworthiness of the Bible, the historicity of Jesus's resurrection from the dead, the reconciliation of modern science with faith in God, and the contradictory truth claims of the world's various religions. Based upon extensive study, we are fully satisfied that there are logical and compelling answers to every objection raised by genuine truth-seekers.

I begin each chapter, following which Mary contributes her thoughts. While the stories we recount will undoubtedly be different from those of many readers, we believe the challenges we have faced and overcome have broad applicability. Reflecting our confidence in the Christian worldview, we quote the Bible throughout this book, since its content is the foundation supporting our beliefs. In the following pages, we will unpack how our relationship with Jesus Christ helped us answer all four of the foregoing questions in the affirmative.

To discover how you too can experience genuine fulfillment, please see the appendix before, during, or after you read this book. We pray you too will make the decision to accept Jesus's offer of a relationship with him, leading to a life filled with purpose, peace, and hope!

One

WHAT IS THE PURPOSE OF MY LIFE?

> You have made us for your-
> self, Lord, and our hearts are
> restless until they find
> rest in you.[2]
> —St. Augustine

I CAN BE easily distracted. Whether it's the siren song of LinkedIn, the seemingly urgent demands of my email inbox, or the endless temptations of my YouTube Premium and Netflix subscriptions, there are times when I find it difficult to focus on more important questions.

And by important, I don't mean "What will I have for dinner?" or "Where will I vacation this year?" or "What clothes will I wear to work today?" or countless other similar questions that regularly exercise my mind.

Responsibilities like marriage, children, and work rightly demand priority attention. Without realizing it, though, I had previously permitted these responsibilities and other issues to distract me from considering some very fundamental

> **I had never felt the need to address arguably the biggest question until one day it hit me right between the eyes. What is the purpose of my life?**

---

[2] St. Augustine, *Confessions: A Modern Translation*, trans. Peter Northcutt (Modern Saints, 2025).

questions. Moreover, while it wasn't always smooth sailing, life just worked for me. Can you relate?

In any event, I had never felt the need to address arguably the biggest question until one day it hit me right between the eyes. *What is the purpose of my life?*

A question along this line popped into my head moments after receiving congratulations from Bill Spencer, then-president of Citibank New York, informing me that the bank's board of directors had approved my appointment as vice president. The promotion wasn't just significant to me because of my relative youth and the authority vested in the role; it was also the realization of a personal goal I had set three years earlier.

However, my elation quickly dissipated. The question of purpose precipitated a feeling of discouragement that overshadowed the excitement of promotion. That evening, I tried to rekindle the celebratory mood with a few drinks.

After all the sacrifice, I suddenly found myself questioning the meaning behind the corporate race I had been running.

THE BACKSTORY

In pursuit of advancement, I had put my family through a lot of disruption, including three big interprovincial and international moves over a short timeframe. In some cases, we didn't even get around to unpacking boxes before we moved again! Yet after all the sacrifice, I suddenly found myself questioning the meaning behind this corporate race.

Up to that point, I would have characterized my life, both professional and personal, as successful and fulfilling. I had always outperformed, both academically and professionally. My personal life was happy, thanks to my wonderful wife Mary and our two (now four) wonderful children. My trajectory was a seemingly continuous sequence of positive milestones that always brought satisfaction.

But I suddenly found myself wondering whether I was missing the deeper meaning of my life. While unaware of St. Augustine at the time, I would have strongly related to his foregoing comment about our restless hearts.

About a year prior to our family's first move with Citibank from Toronto to Montreal, Mary had a dramatic encounter with Jesus Christ that deeply satisfied her search for meaning and fulfillment. Shortly after this encounter, she shared her experience with me one evening over dinner.

I was momentarily stunned. Gathering my wits, I said something to the effect of "Does this mean you're going to stand on a corner in downtown Toronto and hand out Bibles?" My admittedly crude response might have seemed sarcastic, but it was really just my shocked reaction to the genuine change I saw in Mary. She positively exuded the fulfillment she was experiencing. Jesus had become incredibly real to her, and the powerful change in her demeanor was obvious. Over the following weeks, she exhibited a new joy, peace, excitement, and confidence as she studied her Bible and attended a nearby church.

While pleased for Mary, I regarded her decision as having no direct relevance to my own life and, in particular, my career. I viewed the latter as a continuous process of setting and exceeding goals, thereby earning raises, bonuses, and promotions. Since this process was, at the time, satisfying, I felt no need to step back and reassess my life.

Yet when the president of Citibank announced my promotion, I experienced a startling feeling of emptiness. Regardless, I put on a brave front and didn't share my inner struggle with anyone.

Privately, however, I became more and more preoccupied with the true meaning of my life.

A few months later, I accepted yet another promotion as Citibank's head of corporate banking for eastern Canada, based in Montreal. Some time after the family joined me in Montreal, two major Canadian banks approached me concurrently with attractive executive offers. Perhaps it was the-grass-is-always-greener-on-the-other-side-of-the-fence syndrome, but the offers had a certain appeal.

Late in the year, I accepted an offer and made plans to move back to Toronto early the next year. The excitement of career advancement notwithstanding, I remained unfulfilled in the deepest sense and was open to new ideas.

THE CULMINATION OF MY QUEST FOR MEANING

Shortly before Christmas and just prior to our move back to Toronto, Mary asked whether I would like to join her and our children at church that day. In light of my growing receptivity to exploring the question of meaning, I accepted her invitation. However, I was dubious about the benefits and said so. Mary had no problem with my skepticism and off we went.

That day, the young assistant pastor at the neighborhood church began his sermon with a challenge. After listing several possible reasons for attending church—including, for example, to demonstrate moral virtue—he suggested that none of these reasons would win God's favor. He then encouraged anyone who was attending primarily for the reasons he cited to consider leaving. Immediately, some folks got up and left! Until then, I had held the largely uninformed view that most Christians were concerned with virtue signaling. Yet here was this pastor calling them out! His credibility with me shot up. He had my full attention.

The following Sunday, Mary had no difficulty persuading me to join her at church. After the opening prayers and hymns, the senior pastor got up to speak.

At some point during his message, I distinctly heard the words "I am alive," and they weren't coming from the pulpit! In an instant, I knew with certainty that the speaker was Jesus and that those three little words were absolutely true.

Experiencing the reality of God's presence, I felt overwhelmed. Moreover, it seemed obvious to me that since Jesus was alive, he was God. Logically, and we mathematicians love logic, that would mean that God himself wanted a personal relationship with me.

At that moment, it was truly the offer I couldn't refuse! I decided on the spot to obey him in whatever he wanted me to do. In essence, I realized that my quest for meaning and purpose had been answered. My purpose was to be in relationship with Jesus and live for him.

Prior to that day, my knowledge of the Christian worldview hadn't gone much beyond hearing a few Bible verses growing up. But in that moment, I became absolutely certain that God existed and wanted a relationship with me right then, just as I was. It was as though a switch had been pulled inside me and I was a completely different person.

Subsequently, after reading the following excerpt from the apostle Paul's letter to the church at Corinth, I understood what had happened to me: *"This means that anyone who belongs to Christ has become a new person. The old life is gone; a new life has begun!"* (2 Corinthians 5:17, NLT). It is no exaggeration to say that everything changed.

In the days after, I experienced a continual awareness of God's presence wherever I was. Although I didn't yet understand where this newfound faith in God was taking me, I did know with certainty that I was destined to spend eternity with him.

C.S. Lewis, Christian author and former atheist, put it this way: "If we find ourselves with a desire that nothing in this world can satisfy, the most probable explanation is that we were made for another world."[3]

I discovered a unique intimacy with God that cannot be found in any other relationship, even in a strong marriage. I began to wonder whether he wanted me to make a wholesale life change. How could he possibly want me to continue in the corporate world? Should I not be doing something more spiritual?

After wrestling with these questions, however, Mary and I decided to move back to Toronto so I could take up my new position with the bank.

Other aspects of my life changed in short order. Up to that time, I had been drinking a lot. I think it was one of my ways of dealing with stress and dissatisfaction.

[3] C.S. Lewis, *Mere Christianity* (New York, NY: MacMillan Publishing Company, 1952), 106.

When I turned my life over to God, though, the desire for alcohol completely left me, and it was years before I felt the liberty to enjoy any alcoholic beverages.

In addition, my attitude toward money changed immediately. For some reason, fear of financial lack had resulted in a tight-fisted attitude when it came to generosity. While the fear didn't disappear immediately, I experienced a radically new desire to give, and Mary and I began a journey of generosity that has continued to this day.

Life from that point on wasn't always smooth sailing, but I experienced an unexplainable peace through various storms, including business reversals and a cancer diagnosis upon which we will later elaborate. The principal reason is that to this day I have never lost the very real sense of God's intimate presence, whether in my personal life or in business leadership. After prayerful reflection, my life purpose statement became to know Jesus better and to better make him known.

REFLECTIONS ON THE PURPOSE OF LIFE

How about you? Sound familiar? Given all the demands on your life, have you ever paused to consider its purpose? In my experience, this big question tends to get asked only in times of crisis. In my case, it was a positive crisis of success, although it can also be a negative one.

Let's dive into the following three important questions concerning the purpose of life:

1. Is purpose a product of mind or chance?
2. If purpose is a product of mind, whose mind?
3. What are the implications of a God-determined purpose?

Purpose is a product of mind. According to Merriam-Webster, the word purpose may be defined as "something set up as an object or end to be attained."[4] For example, it can be used in conjunction with purposeful activities to support a specific goal, such as training to run a marathon or the raison d'être of an organization as set forth in its mission statement.

Both the foregoing purposes are sub-ultimate; that is, they may be established by individuals or organizations without regard to the big personal question "Why do I exist in the first place?" This latter question relates to the ultimate purpose of our lives, which is also captured by the question "What is the meaning of my life?"

With due respect to those who advocate for the view that our choices are predetermined by mysterious forces beyond our control, let's go with common sense!

Common sense tells us that statements of goals and purpose are products of mind rather than chance or predetermination. However, there are some individuals, particularly within the scientific community, who maintain that this common sense understanding is incorrect. They claim that reality can only be understood in material terms such as electrons, protons, and neutrons. By extension, some would say that we don't really have free choice, that free choice is an illusion since our actions are predetermined in some mysterious way that cannot be articulated. It's an interesting hypothesis that, as far as I'm aware, lacks evidential support.

---

[4] "Purpose," *Merriam-Webster*. Date of access: May 24, 2025 (https://www.merriam-webster.com/dictionary/purpose).

As human beings, we exercise free choice to come up with goals that establish where we're going. These in turn can be used to inform action plans, including business and personal strategies.

Just as statements of goals and strategies are products of mind, so too are statements of purpose. In the business setting, corporate purpose is typically captured in mission statements. They're often framed like this: "Our mission [a.k.a. purpose] is to help [so-and-so] by doing [such-and-such]."

That said, what about the purpose of my life as distinct from the purpose of the organization I serve? What was I made for? Common sense tells us that our purpose must be the product of mind, since random forces don't make choices to achieve a specific objective. By definition, they simply can't be purposeful.

Whose mind determines purpose? If our purpose is the product of mind, the question becomes, "Whose mind?" When it comes to ultimate purpose, there are only two possible sources: external or internal. Either it is determined externally by the creator of everything, including humankind, or internally by ourselves. There are no other alternatives.

If God created us, it is only logical that he did so for some specific ultimate purpose that only he can reveal. According to the apostle Paul, *"we know that in all things God works for the good of those who love him, who have been called according to his purpose"* (Romans 8:28, NIV).

By analogy, a car doesn't establish its own purpose. Rather, it is the inventor who, with the goal of creating a superior mode of transport, designed the car to achieve that end. Put differently, the car didn't determine its own meaning!

By contrast, if there is at bottom no creator outside ourselves, we are left to our own devices when attempting to answer this question. As it happens, the reality is that most individuals in the West are functional atheists. While they may say they believe God exists, they conduct their lives completely indifferent to his plans and purposes for them. And by extension, most people of this mindset tend not to think in terms of ultimate purpose.

The conclusion that there is no ultimate purpose is entirely consistent with the materialistic worldview that asserts we are the end-product of chance operating on matter over time. Thus, people of this mindset would resonate with the perspective of Richard Dawkins, Oxford biologist and outspoken atheist, who declared, "The universe that we observe has precisely the properties we should expect if there is, at bottom, no design, no purpose, no evil, no good, nothing but blind, pitiless indifference."[5]

Dawkin's assertion doesn't stand up to critical scrutiny by many of his fellow scientists. Rather, it is anchored firmly in his materialistic worldview.

Folks in this camp tend not to ruminate over things ultimate. We might infer from their lives, however, that their self-defined ultimate purpose is to maximize their personal happiness. By definition, this approach is "me-centric."

The secular orientation begins with the objective of survival but doesn't end there. It likely includes other sources of happiness,

---

[5] Richard Dawkins, *River Out of Eden: A Darwinian View of Life* (New York, NY: Basic Books, 2008), 134.

such as public recognition, health, wealth, family, friendships, and even involvement in charitable activities. While laudable, the latter are ultimately to the benefit of the giver in terms of personal satisfaction (a.k.a. happiness).

In conclusion, the question regarding the source of our ultimate purpose is the biggest and arguably most important question we could ever ask. If we haven't asked this question yet, we are by default operating on the basis that we are the authors of our own purpose. And this assumption, whether acknowledged or not, informs all our choices.

What are the implications of my God-determined purpose? A fundamental corollary of the view that our purpose is God-determined is that it must be discovered through his disclosure rather than formulated by us. Put differently, it comes to us by way of revelation rather than thoughtful analysis.

While applying our minds to critical thinking is an important dimension of living well, we must connect with God at the spiritual level since he is spirit. For example, I didn't encounter God as the result of a thought process. Rather, he revealed himself to me and I needed no further proof of his existence. Since that first encounter, I knew that I knew him; the certainty of that knowledge has never left me, even during the hard times. This truth derives from the apostle Paul's letter to the early church in Rome, which declares that I know God by the witness of his indwelling Spirit with my spirit (Romans 8:16).

Once I discovered that my purpose was determined by God and would unfold as I followed his leading, the restlessness that accompanied my search for meaning dissipated. Moreover, I became much more aware of the implications of his involvement in my life. This new awareness was based upon biblical revelation concerning who he is, what he has accomplished on my behalf, and what he has determined for me and my future. This latter implication feeds into the subsequent discussion of fulfillment, peace, and hope in the inevitable ups and downs of life.

GOD'S NATURE UNDERSCORES THE IMPORTANCE OF OUR PURPOSE

Think about it! The creator of everything, including us, has a specific purpose in mind for each and every one of us.

According to the Bible, God is perfect in all his ways (Psalm 18:30). This means, among other things, that he is all-powerful, all-knowing, all-loving, all-just, and all-good. He is holy beyond our comprehension. His multifaceted perfection, and we've just scraped the surface, infuses our lives with divine importance.

Indeed, the meaning of our lives is inextricably bound up in his purpose for each of us.

WHAT GOD DID FOR US UNDERSCORES HIS LOVE

As discussed in the appendix, God himself suffered more than any human has ever suffered on behalf of another. As the Son of God, Jesus bore the punishment we each deserve for our failures to obey God's will. This includes indifference toward him and disregard for his plans and purposes in creating us.

By offering himself on the cross in our place, Jesus satisfied the requirements of justice. He bore our punishment and opened the door to a relationship with God to all who receive his offer of forgiveness and allow him to direct their lives.

To rescue us, Jesus endured unimaginable personal suffering.

First, while Jesus was totally innocent under Mosaic law, the religious leaders, both envious and afraid of his growing popularity, found him guilty of blasphemy and sentenced him to death. He suffered terrible injustice.

Second, Jesus underwent a separation from God the Father as all of humanity's sin—past, present, and future—and the consequences of that sin were laid on him (1 Peter 2:24). It's difficult for us to imagine the pain Jesus experienced when, for one and only one time, he was separated from God the Father.

Third, he was betrayed by one of his closest friends, abandoned by the rest, and mocked by the very people he had come to rescue through his self-substitutionary sacrifice.

Fourth and finally, the physical pain he endured, both prior to and during the crucifixion, is incomprehensible, resulting in the coining of a new word: excruciating.

The immeasurable magnitude of Jesus's suffering underscores God's love for each of us and the incalculable importance he places on each of our lives and, by extension, his unique purpose in creating us.

WHAT GOD SAYS ABOUT US EMPOWERS OUR PURPOSE

God created us in his image and for his purpose. Often, however, we forget who we are and avoid purpose-related actions out of fear of negative repercussions. The Bible declares that as we seek first to do his will—to carry out his purpose in creating us—he will take care of the rest, including providing for all our needs (Matthew 6:33). Thus, almighty God empowers us to achieve our purpose.

That said, he honors us as his image-bearers by granting us the freedom to choose whether to obey his call on our lives.

MARY ADDS

> Do not marvel that I said to you,
> "You must be born again."[6]
> —Jesus

Early in my professional career as a physiotherapist, I poured through the four Gospels in the New Testament (the biographies of Jesus Christ) as well as a vivid commentary on the life of Jesus which included a medical assessment of the suffering he endured on the cross for me and every person ever born.

The catalyst for this investigation was some conversations with Tom, a physiotherapy patient, who provoked me to revisit my childhood faith. I had spent my childhood and youth in Anglican churches and had even been baptized and confirmed as a teenager.

Even though I had experienced God's presence many times over those years, I didn't have the assurance of being loved and accepted by him.

Tom was a passionate follower of Jesus. As we discussed certain new age philosophies I had been studying, he expressed concern for me. While I hadn't found any peace in these occultic explorations, I didn't mention that to Tom.

---

[6] John 3:7, ESV.

As it happens, prior to these conversations a quiet voice inside me had asked, "Who made the heavens, the stars, and the planets?"

"You did, Lord!" I immediately whispered.

At that moment, I understood that my investigation of astrology and other alternative religions was taking me down the wrong path.

As a young father, Tom was especially interested in studying Hebrew texts and had made several connections with Toronto's Jewish community. He referred to a few verses in the Old Testament that prescribed the stoning of false prophets.

That certainly got my attention! At the time of our conversation, there were a few self-proclaimed "prophets" whose columns appeared daily in many leading newspapers. Of course, he wasn't suggesting that stoning be meted out today! Rather, he was warning that these prophecies were not from God, nor were they based upon his revelation as recorded in the Bible.

He also pointed out that there is a real spiritual realm that could bring harm and oppression to me as a result of dabbling in the occult.

My encounter with Tom was a setup by God to point me to the truth! As a result of these daily conversations during his weekday treatments, I determined to conduct my own study of the Bible, both the Old and New Testaments. During the month I treated him, I began to voraciously read my Bible and study books from the local library on the life and ministry of Jesus.

One morning while our two-year-old daughter Skye was at a nearby nursery school, I was impressed to kneel and pray in our bedroom. From my heart, I spoke to Jesus and asked him to forgive me. While I had spent years at church, I had never appreciated that he is exactly who he says he is, that he died for me and had risen from the dead, that he truly is the Son of God. In my mind, I imagined taking Skye with me to the local church so we could learn about God together.

In a split second, however, I sensed the presence of Jesus in the room with me and realized with certainty that he is alive! He was speaking to me, filling my heart and my whole being with his love.

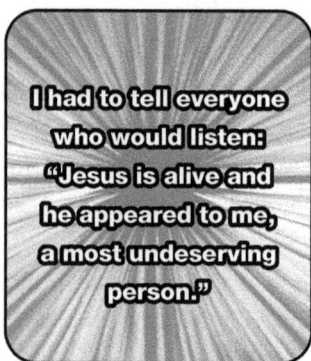

> I had to tell everyone who would listen: "Jesus is alive and he appeared to me, a most undeserving person."

Tears of joy welled up and I lay on the floor for a long time, allowing his presence to flood my whole being! How could I have missed this truth over so many years and a great education!

I had to tell everyone who would listen: "Jesus is alive and he appeared to me, a most undeserving person." His Spirit prompted me to read the Bible, especially the New Testament. I devoured a contemporary translation I had bought as a teenager. My craving for his Word and desire to know him filled me with purpose immediately. I even read my Bible on the subway trip to and from work! I didn't care who saw me.

As the apostle Paul wrote to the early church in Colossae, God *"has delivered [me] from the power of darkness and conveyed [me] into the kingdom of the Son of His love, in whom*

[I] have redemption through His blood, the forgiveness of sins" (Colossians 1:13–14, NKJV).

My search for the meaning of my life was over. My life's purpose was to know Jesus and to make him known!

WAKE-UP CALL

Many years ago, we prayerfully wrote down our life purpose statement, which is to know Jesus better and to better make him known. We challenge you to ask God about his purpose for your life. It's only common sense to ask this question of the one who designed you for his purposes. As we shall address in the next chapter, the answer to this question opens the door to a truly fulfilling life!

Two

AM I LIVING A FULFILLED LIFE?

I have come that they may
have life, and have it
to the full.[7]
—Jesus

RECOGNIZING THAT WE are each unique and that readers need to discover their own God-given purpose and accompanying action plan, I will now provide some examples of how living out these two aspects of my life purpose statement has brought me fulfillment.

KNOWING JESUS BETTER

When I first encountered Jesus, I knew virtually nothing about him in the sense of head knowledge. At that moment, however, I knew him *relationally*. I surrendered my life to him on the spot and God placed his Holy Spirit in me. According to the Bible, I then knew Jesus by the witness of his indwelling Holy Spirit (1 Corinthians 6:19).

Given my general propensity to intellectualize issues, I find it interesting (if not humorous) that God bypassed my intellect completely when Jesus revealed himself to me. As the apostle Paul wrote in his letter to the early church in Rome,

> You, however, are not in the realm of the flesh
> but are in the realm of the Spirit, if indeed the
> Spirit of God lives in you. And if anyone does not

[7] John 10:10, NIV.

have the Spirit of Christ, they do not belong to Christ. But if Christ is in you, then even though your body is subject to death because of sin, the Spirit gives life because of righteousness. And if the Spirit of him who raised Jesus from the dead is living in you, he who raised Christ from the dead will also give life to your mortal bodies because of his Spirit who lives in you. (Romans 8:9–11, NIV)

> For me, knowing Jesus better revolves around making my relationship with him the primary driver of both my personal and professional life.

For me, knowing Jesus better revolves around making my relationship with him the primary driver of both my personal and professional life.

With every passing day, my knowledge of Jesus grows as Mary and I spend quiet times together worshiping God, reading the Bible, and praying over our lives and those of our family and various acquaintances, including neighbors and those we know through business, church, and charity. God's presence remains with us throughout the day as we go about our various responsibilities.

Being purpose-driven, our normal daily activities produce genuine fulfillment each and every day. Very importantly, these activities include encouraging our children and grandchildren in numerous ways.

MAKING JESUS KNOWN

According to the Bible, every follower of Jesus is called to be his ambassador to the world. Merriam-Webster defines an ambassador as "a diplomatic agent of the highest rank accredited to a foreign government or sovereign as the resident representative of his or her own government or sovereign."[8] Based upon this definition, followers of Jesus are authorized representatives of the kingdom of God's rule, dispatched into the world at large.

In that role, my responsibility is twofold—first, to represent God well in all my personal and professional conduct, and second, to help others understand God's plan for humanity in general and them in particular. In this way, I partner with God's Holy Spirit by helping others recognize and satisfy their need for a relationship with their creator and thereby themselves becoming members of the kingdom of God.

Put differently, my ambassadorial role is to make Jesus known to others, facilitating a growing number of Jesus's followers on earth.

Regarding representing God well to others, the apostle Paul encourages followers of Jesus to imitate God in every situation (Ephesians 5:1–2). Imitation is multifaceted, including being mission-focused, serving others, demonstrating humility, telling the truth even when it hurts, persisting in the face of challenges, inspiring courage in others, making wise choices, attributing success to teammates, and protecting those around us.

Here's a personal example regarding ethical conduct. Very early in my Christian walk, I led a project finance team at an international

[8] "Ambassador," *Merriam-Webster*. Date of access: May 24, 2025 (https://www.merriam-webster.com/dictionary/ambassador).

bank. That year, the CEO of the bank issued an edict to the effect that, as part of a cost-cutting drive, the bank wouldn't fund staff Christmas parties. Notwithstanding, one of my senior staff suggested that we hold the annual Christmas event but characterize it as "client entertaining."

In light of the CEO's directive, I said no!

Shortly thereafter, I found myself in the office of the senior executive to whom my boss reported. He asked why I wouldn't support the bank-funded Christmas party. In response, I told him that I was a follower of Jesus and, as such, couldn't condone any unethical conduct. He accepted my response.

That year, we paid for our own Christmas party and I was left with the distinct impression that my decision wasn't popular with other members of my group!

On another occasion, I was confronted by a member of the senior management team of the venture capital company I led. He was very upset that I had met with the chief investment officer (CIO) of one of Canada's largest life insurance companies, which was a unitholder in our venture capital fund. This individual felt strongly that he should have been invited to accompany me, since he had introduced the CIO to our company and played a role in securing the company's investment in our fund.

I had neglected to invite him because I had a previous relationship with the CIO, dating back to the days when he and I had both held executive positions at a major Canadian bank.

Recognizing that my colleague had a valid point, I immediately asked him to forgive me, since Jesus commands us not only to forgive but to ask forgiveness when we have wronged others. He was so taken aback, perhaps thinking I would pull the CEO card, that he muttered something along the lines of "Fine" and departed.

Since I had told him previously that I was a follower of Jesus, I hope he connected my asking forgiveness with my self-proclaimed identity.

For me, representing God well to others includes, most importantly, explicitly sharing my faith in Jesus, including not only those I encounter in my professional life but everyone I meet. In this regard, I believe that transparency is the best policy. Regardless of the social rank of those with whom I engage personally or professionally, I seek early opportunities to let them know I am a follower of Jesus. This personal rule applies whether the other person is a friend, neighbor, service provider, or CEO of a large company. By letting people know early on that I am a follower of Jesus, I make myself accountable to them and open the door to future discussions through which I can glorify God by my words and conduct.

Importantly, I don't tell them that I'm a Christian, since most people don't know what a Christian is! The Christian worldview is based entirely on biblical revelation, but most people are biblically illiterate, particularly in advanced Western economies. As a result, they often form their perspective on Christianity based on unflattering stories in the media about the Christian worldview, the misbehavior of people they understand to be Christians, or both.

Jesus is the greatest example of excellence and I believe I am called to imitate him by conducting myself with excellence. In business, this includes loving other stakeholders in my business, such as employees, vendors, creditors, and shareholders. I aim to accomplish this goal by treating them as I would want to be treated. It also includes being known as a man of my word, even in seemingly small matters like turning up before a meeting is scheduled to begin.

I've learned that practicing excellence in all my professional affairs increases my credibility when I step out and explicitly share about my faith in God with others, particularly my marketplace peers. Outside the business realm, this desire to conduct myself with excellence motivates my words and actions.

That said, I sometimes fall short of this goal.

> My three rules for explicitly sharing my faith in God with others are to listen, listen, and listen!

My three rules for explicitly sharing my faith in God with others are to listen, listen, and listen! By carefully paying attention when others speak, I not only honor them but also learn about challenges they're facing, and these are often challenges that I and other believers I know have also faced. As a result, doors frequently open to sharing how Jesus has answered prayers. Typically I ask for permission to pray for them and I've never had anyone say no.

The most important message I seek to communicate, whenever possible, is that a relationship with Jesus opens the door to purpose, peace, and hope in this life and ultimately to eternal life in his presence.

The following comment by Penn Jillette in a video blog published in 2010 is often on my mind when I interact with others: "How much do you have to hate somebody to believe that everlasting life is possible and not tell them that?"[9] It's ironic that Jillette, an outspoken atheist, is the one to draw the logical conclusion that not sharing the good news with others is the epitome of hatred if we Christians truly believe everlasting life in the presence of God is possible.

REFLECTIONS ON FULFILLMENT

One would be hard-pressed to find anyone in the me-centric camp who would say with conviction that they're both happy and fulfilled. As per C.S. Lewis's earlier quote, nothing seems to satisfy their deepest desires.

Typically, we experience a measure of fulfillment when we achieve a goal or dream. For example, I felt a burst of enjoyment when, as a young man, I achieved my goal of becoming a vice president of Citibank and, prior to that, completing my first twenty-six-mile marathon.

These types of fulfillment, while pleasurable, are short-lived, analogous to the brief pleasure of a vacation in the midst of a busy career. As many of us have discovered, the positive feelings that accompany vacations often dissipate quickly when we return to the busyness of the so-called real world.

Discovering the purpose of our lives is a necessary but insufficient condition to experiencing fulfillment. The key to finding fulfillment is acting out our purpose. Put differently, we need to treat our purpose as the organizing principle for our activities, which might be expressed mathematically as:

$$purpose + purpose\text{-}driven\ action = fulfillment$$

---

[9] "A Gift of a Bible," *YouTube*. July 8, 2010 (https://www.youtube.com/watch?v=6md638s-mQd8&ab_channel=beinzee).

Until we discover the ultimate purpose of our lives, fulfillment isn't only elusive but, in the end, unachievable. And goals reached based on internally created purpose statements, including those couched in virtuous language, won't produce lasting fulfillment.

For example, prior to my encounter with Jesus, I experienced discouragement rather than fulfillment after I achieved a big professional goal. After that encounter, by contrast, my question concerning the meaning of my own life was instantly resolved! From that moment on, the meaning (purpose) of my life became to know Jesus better and to better make him known. These two distinct aspects of my personal purpose statement require action to realize them. And as I pursue them, I experience genuine fulfillment.

MARY ADDS

> Now this is eternal life: that they know you,
> the only true God, and Jesus Christ,
> whom you have sent.[10]
> —Jesus

The door to fulfillment opened wide for me when I accepted Jesus's invitation to believe in him and his work on my behalf. As a result, I crossed the threshold into an intimate relationship with him, becoming an entirely new creation through the power of the Holy Spirit (2 Corinthians 5:17).

It was almost as though I had come out of darkness into a brightly lit room! As I read my Bible, the Holy Spirit illuminated the meaning and application of what I was reading and I grew daily in

---

[10] John 17:3, NIV.

my knowledge of God. Connecting regularly with other believers in Jesus, as well as conversing with and responding to God, also helped me grow in my relationship with him.

That said, I definitely didn't change overnight, and to this day I often encounter challenges needing his wisdom, love, and restraint.

This new relationship impacted every aspect of my life, including my marriage to Garth; my role as a mother and grandmother to our wonderful family of four children, their spouses, and nine grandchildren; and my work and other activities outside the home. Relating with others as a follower of Jesus has been immeasurably fulfilling for me, including sharing the good news of Jesus in some way wherever I find myself.

Very early in my new faith journey, I was impressed that, since Jesus never changes (Hebrews 13:8), he wants to use me to heal others just as he acted through his followers during his earthly ministry.

> Very early in my new faith journey, I was impressed that, since Jesus never changes (Hebrews 13:8), he wants to use me to heal others just as he acted through his followers during his earthly ministry.

In a story recounted in Luke's gospel, Jesus authorizes and empowers his followers to heal people, and when they returned with exciting success stories Jesus rejoiced and commended them for their childlike faith (Luke 10:9, 17–21).

These stories and many others encouraged me to believe that he wanted to work through me in the healing realm. His calling on my life wasn't based upon my own godliness or personal power.

Rather, it was based on Jesus authorizing me and all believers to demonstrate his love, compassion, and power by healing the sick in his name.

While Garth and I have many testimonies of supernatural healing, here are two.

KENYA

As part of a teaching team from our church, we stayed at the Rift Valley Cricket Club north of Nairobi in the city of Nakuru. One day, four of us were sitting by the club pool when a tall, elegant woman walked by with great difficulty. We all felt concern for the obvious pain she was experiencing and asked her for permission to pray. The woman, whose name was Zia, agreed immediately and sat in a garden chair on the pool deck.

She tearfully explained that she'd been in a single-car accident that had destroyed her car and left her with several fractures. Following surgery, she was immobilized in a body cast for nine months. This traumatic accident had left her in a state of physical and emotional suffering.

We prayed first for the fear that had engulfed her, then for emotional comfort, and finally for the healing of her body. As we prayed, she experienced peace and cried tears of joy.

After standing, she said that she felt much better and hugged each one of us. When I asked whether the pain had completely gone, she said that it hadn't but it had definitely lessened. I then asked the Holy Spirit what to say next, and from my lips tumbled words to the effect that she would be healed as she went.

Upon walking about fifteen feet, Zia stopped and screamed. She had been completely set free from pain!

I explained to her that she had been healed in Jesus's name. When asked whether she knew Jesus, she said that she didn't but would like to then and there.

As it happens, she was a Muslim! We explained the Gospel and prayed with her to receive Jesus's gift of salvation. Zia did and positively radiated joy! After this, we introduced her to the rest of our team, including our pastors, and she spent some time with all of us.

CANADA

One morning as I was out for a run in our Greater Toronto Area neighborhood, I felt impressed by the Holy Spirit to return home and drive to our local butcher shop before 9:30 a.m. This prompting seemed somewhat urgent and I wondered what the Lord had in mind.

As I went to the cash register to purchase a few items, Kelly, a longtime employee, greeted me tearfully.

"Mary, I'm in so much back pain," she said. "I have to go home immediately after checking you out."

Experiencing a surge of boldness, I asked whether I could pray for her right there and then. She replied that she was undeserving of prayer, but I assured her that God loved her and wanted her to be healed. With that, she agreed to be prayed for.

Stepping behind the counter, I asked permission to lay my hand on her back.

"Anything!" she replied.

As I took authority over the pain and underlying problem in the name of Jesus, all the pain left immediately and her mobility was restored. We both began to praise Jesus right there in the store and she went on to tell anyone who would listen about Jesus that very day! After I left, she called her mother to share this good news.

A few days later, as a long weekend approached, I returned to the store to pick up some steaks for a barbecue and check up on Kelly. As soon as she saw me, she began shouting about how Jesus had healed her. She told everyone in the store, including her employer, Frank, who by then had heard her testimony several times!

This particular store wasn't large, so everyone there could hear Kelly rejoicing and giving glory to Jesus with a childlike attitude. It gave me great personal fulfillment to see Kelly share about her healing and the name of Jesus with such passion and transparency!

WAKE-UP CALL

Do you wake up each day knowing why you exist and where you're going? Have you ever achieved a big goal and then found yourself wondering whether there's more to life?

If you answered no to the first question or yes to the second, perhaps it's time to think outside the box.

As someone once said, insanity can be defined as doing the same thing over and over again while expecting a different outcome! For an altogether different approach to life, leading to meaning and fulfillment, please see the appendix.

Three

DO I HAVE INNER PEACE IN THE MIDST OF TURMOIL?

You will keep in perfect
peace those whose minds are
steadfast, because they
trust in you.[11]
—Prophet Isaiah

IN HIS LETTER to the early church, the apostle Peter encourages them as follows: *"Cast all your anxiety on him [God] because he cares for you"* (1 Peter 5:7, NIV). Mary and I could cite many examples where we've done so and, as a result, experienced his peace, a feeling of calm that exceeds any peace possible from worldly solutions. Indeed, when we've cast our worries upon him, his peace has invariably flooded our hearts!

The following are personal examples of experiencing his peace in the midst of storms.

FINANCIAL CHALLENGES

My parents lived through the Great Depression. A corporate lawyer, my father had a flair for risk-taking in the mining business, including funding prospectors' highly speculative claim-staking ventures. By contrast, my mother specialized in risk avoidance. Her cautious attitude was based not only upon her family's experiences during the Great Depression but also my father's penchant for risk-taking!

---

[11] Isaiah 26:3, NIV.

To mitigate the risk of running out of cash, my mother implemented tight budgetary controls. One of my strongest childhood memories was the annual purchase of clothing for me and my siblings before the school year began. She would buy two new changes of clothes for each of us and required that they last for the entire year. As you might imagine, we took good care of our streamlined wardrobes!

I carried her fear of financial lack into our marriage. My philosophy was that our family's financial well-being rested entirely on my shoulders. As a result, I instituted tight budgetary controls on our spending to ensure we lived within our means and avoided borrowing. I reasoned that if something went wrong with our finances, I could only look to myself for solutions.

This philosophy also led me to avoid financial generosity in favor of meeting our physical needs and accumulating savings.

Following my encounter with Jesus, I experienced a new spirit of generosity and we immediately began giving a material amount of our before-tax income to our church and other worthy causes. Since I still believed in living within a budget, we funded our generosity from the increase in compensation that accompanied my acceptance of an executive position with a major Canadian bank.

Here are two financial reversal stories in which God's peace saw us through a dark valley.

Negative net worth. A few years after I turned my life over to Jesus, Mary launched a marketing business. It quickly gained traction, and as a result we decided that I would join her with the goal of not only supporting our family but also creating wealth over time.

Importantly, this decision was taken only after much due diligence and prayer, since we were both committed to proceeding only if God validated the decision. Because the success of this new venture was contingent on both Mary's and my full-time commitment, I resigned from my leadership role in the investment management firm I had joined following my corporate banking days.

Looking back on this decision, I shake my head. We went from the relative comfort of a corporate leadership role, with some measure of financial security based upon past performance and the firm's positive outlook, to starting a new business which by definition involved serious financial risk. That said, we were confident of God's willingness and ability to provide for all our needs (Matthew 6:33) and sacrificed financially to build the new venture.

To fund our startup expenses, we sold our home in a beautiful (and expensive) area of Toronto and rented another home elsewhere in the city. Since we sold during a significant real estate meltdown, we incurred a large financial loss. While the business did grow a lot over a couple of years, it wasn't sufficiently profitable to meet the growing needs of our six-member family and the negative cashflow ate up the proceeds from the sale of our house.

Ultimately, I accepted an offer to return to my former company for the sake of the family. By this time we were wondering whether we would ever be able to buy another house.

Prior to my decision to join Mary in the new marketing venture, our personal net worth had been significant for our stage of life and it was growing. After two years, it was negative!

Notwithstanding the significant financial challenges we endured, we never lost sight of the reality that God was watching over us. He would see us through. Thus, even in the midst of such worrying circumstances, we experienced God's peace.

The Great Recession. From late 2007 to the middle of 2009, the entire world went through what has been labelled the Great Recession. Financial markets melted down and some major institutions failed.

As an investment management firm, we weren't immune and the portfolios we managed went through a period of unprecedented volatility. Through it all, the deep peace of God inside me was on display to those around me.

Ultimately, we emerged from the Great Recession stronger than ever and in due course I sold my interest in the firm to my partners. God saw us through and along the way created financial resources for us to steward!

PEACE IN THE MIDST OF A HEALTH CRISIS

Several years ago, my doctor called to discuss my annual chest X-ray, which showed a small growth on my right lung. He mentioned the possibility of some sort of infection stemming from a trip to Ghana a few weeks prior.

To better understand what was going on, however, he referred me to a respirologist. Shortly thereafter, the respirologist launched me on a multifaceted and lengthy diagnostic journey to determine the nature of the growth.

Several months later, he told me that the only way to definitively determine whether the growth was benign or cancerous was to undergo a lung biopsy. After the biopsy, I travelled to Europe for several days on business. Upon my return, the respirologist's office called to arrange an appointment at my earliest convenience.

A man of few words, my doctor opened with these chilling words: "You have lung cancer." After this disconcerting revelation, he added that the cancer was relatively early stage, lending itself to surgical intervention.

As it happened, one of Toronto's top thoracic surgeons was in the hospital that day. From my perspective, this fortuitous circumstance was an example of God's providence.

Within an hour of my receiving the diagnosis, we met and he explained the procedure in some detail. Subject to further procedures to ensure the cancer hadn't spread further, he told me that he would perform the surgery about ten days hence.

For most people, "You have cancer" are the scariest words they can hear. While I didn't rejoice at the news, neither did I experience fear. Indeed, the peace of God enveloped me.

Confident that my life was in God's hands, I rested in his peace throughout those days leading up to the surgery. In fact, Mary and I enjoyed dinner at a nice restaurant the night before the procedure, which I then came through with flying colors.

Within a relatively short time, I returned home and even resumed my exercise routine.

> For most people, "You have cancer" are the scariest words they can hear. While I didn't rejoice at the news, neither did I experience fear. Indeed, the peace of God enveloped me.

To this day, I thank God for having provided two superb doctors: first, my diligent family doctor whose thorough annual medical examination helped us to address the cancer at an early stage, and second, the brilliant thoracic surgeon who removed the growth using the latest techniques of keyhole surgery.

After regular follow-up appointments for a number of years, my surgeon declared me completely cancer-free!

REFLECTIONS ON PEACE

A common tendency today is to equate peace with the absence of difficulties—including, in the extreme, war. As every one of us can attest, real life is typically a mix of actual or perceived problems interspersed with quieter times. If we succumb to the feelings associated with them, these problems can steal our peace. They range from intermittent bouts of anxiety to short- and long-term troubles including those related to family, relationships, illness, finances, and employment.

These peace-stealers should come as no surprise. Jesus himself declared that life in this world will be full of troubles. However, he went on to assert that the solution to every one of them rests in our relationship with him.

As recorded in John's gospel, Jesus said, *"I have told you these things, so that in me you may have peace. In this world you will have trouble. But take heart! I have overcome the world"* (John 16:33, NIV). Note that he connects our experience of peace with our relationship with him.

When we consider the attributes of God described in the Bible, it becomes clear why peace with God is the only true, ultimate peace. Moreover, it's solely available to those in relationship with him.

According to scripture, God is perfect in all his ways (Psalm 18:30). He is the architect and creator of space, time, energy, and matter. He is the author of all life, including us, whom he created in his image. He is purposeful, all-powerful, all-knowing, and every-where-present. Nothing we experience in our lives comes as a surprise to God, since he knows everything from beginning to end. He is all-loving and the best-ever example of selfless generosity.

When we succumb to his love, receive his forgiveness, and invite him to take charge of our lives, he makes our spirits come alive in him (2 Corinthians 5:17). His Holy Spirit comes to dwell inside us and witnesses to our now-living spirits that we have been reconciled with him, thereby guaranteeing our enjoyment of his presence forever.

Moreover, the Bible declares that the peace of God is one of several fruits of his indwelling presence (Galatians 5:22–23). Thus we can tap into his peace whenever we choose to do so!

MARY ADDS

> Do not be anxious about anything, but in
> every situation, by prayer and petition, with
> thanksgiving, present your requests to God.
> And the peace of God, which transcends all
> understanding, will guard your hearts and
> your minds in Christ Jesus.[12]
> —Apostle Paul

---

[12] Philippians 4:6–7, NIV.

Garth's cancer trial could have been a big peace-stealer for both of us. Indeed, after Garth asked for his initial thoughts on the X-ray anomaly, the respirologist mentioned cancer as one possibility. No sooner had the question tumbled out of Garth's mouth than he heard the Holy Spirit tell him not to worry about the doctor's answer.

Upon hearing about the respirologist's comment, I was naturally very concerned. However, the reassurance Garth received from the Lord really comforted me. Seeing this situation as a faith challenge, we knew that we needed to pray, ask for healing, and focus on God as the ultimate source of our peace.

The foregoing scripture from Paul's letter to the Philippian church was my mainstay over the next several months as Garth underwent treatments, tests, and consultations. Though the growth did not increase in size, neither did it shrink. Moreover, one particularly invasive test resulted in some very worrisome side effects, including a high fever. However, Garth felt generally healthy, had no other symptoms, and kept up his running routine.

We continued to focus on the Lord through worship, prayer, and meditating on passages of the Bible.

One day, while driving to pick up our drycleaning just prior to our annual visit to Barbados, I had a vision from the Lord. He impressed on me to tell Garth that this sickness didn't belong to him because Jesus had personally carried away all his diseases.

The following verses were displayed in living color, and to this day I don't know how I was able to continue driving!

...[Jesus] drove out the spirits with a word and healed all the sick. This was to fulfill what was spoken through the prophet Isaiah: "He took up our infirmities and bore our diseases." (Matthew 8:16–17, NIV)

But he was pierced for our transgressions, he was crushed for our iniquities; the punishment that brought us peace was on him, and by his wounds we are healed. (Isaiah 53:5, NIV)

"He himself bore our sins" in his body on the cross, so that we might die to sins and live for righteousness; "by his wounds you have been healed." (1 Peter 2:24, NIV)

In my heart, I knew that God intended Garth to experience a complete healing. By faith, we continued to command the growth to be torn out by its roots, as Jesus demonstrated when he cursed the fig tree and it withered from the roots (Mark 11:12–14).

When the cancer was finally diagnosed, I experienced perfect peace. Since a leading thoracic surgeon was immediately available to remove the upper lobe of Garth's right lung through keyhole surgery, we received this news as God's providence.

Led by the Holy Spirit, however, we continued to pray for a healing miracle. Notwithstanding, if the final preoperative test didn't confirm that the growth was gone, we agreed to give thanks for God's amazing provision of minimally invasive surgery.

We enjoyed a wonderful steak dinner the night before the scheduled surgery and I felt enveloped by the most tangible peace ever! We talked about our great love for each other and how thankful we were for our lives and family.

Our son Mark drove us to the hospital the next morning and then joined me in the waiting room, as did our entire family. Throughout, I continued to experience God's amazing peace.

As it happens, we arrived late for the surgery, since the hospital had changed the time, but we were unaware of the change as we hadn't checked our voicemail messages! In fact, Garth's late arrival was a blessing in disguise, as he was almost immediately whisked away to the surgery theatre. As he entered the theatre, Garth joked with the medical team: "Have you ever done this before—and if so, what's your track record?"

After an hour and a half, the surgeon visited our family in the waiting room to inform us that the preoperative biopsies confirmed no spread of cancer to the lymph nodes. The Lord had answered our prayers, since any spread would have necessitated chemotherapy prior to proceeding with surgery! Two and a half hours later, the surgeon rejoined us in the waiting room to announce that the procedure had been successful and Garth was already awake and joking with the nurses. We all rejoiced!

A few days later, Garth and I went for a two-kilometer walk through our neighborhood. As the growth had been small and the cancer early stage, we prayerfully decided against any follow-up procedures, including chemotherapy aimed at mitigating the risk of recurrence.

Months later, X-rays confirmed that the lung had regrown to its normal size! Reflecting on this unexpected trial, I can only conclude that the peace I experienced was completely supernatural.

Reflecting on this unexpected trial, I can only conclude that the peace I experienced was completely supernatural.

WAKE-UP CALL

Do you find peace only in the absence of troubles? If peace is elusive, do you occasionally attempt to create it by entertaining yourself, such as binge-watching Netflix or using alcohol or recreational drugs to enhance your mood? We have found that experiencing genuine peace isn't a function of what we do when faced with the inevitable difficulties or when life is going well. Indeed, genuine peace cannot be found in our circumstances or how we deal with them. Rather, it is found exclusively in our relationship with Jesus.

Four

DO I HAVE ANY ULTIMATE HOPE?

> Praise be to the God and
> Father of our Lord Jesus
> Christ! In his great mercy he
> has given us new birth into a
> living hope through the resur-
> rection of Jesus Christ from
> the dead…[13]
> —Apostle Peter

BASED UPON OUR personal knowledge of Jesus, Mary and I have real hope for our future. God created us for eternal relationship with him. Based upon his character, including him being the epitome of truth-telling and various other incomparable attributes, we know that the best comes after we depart our physical bodies.

We echo the apostle Paul, who wrestled with the question of which was better: to remain in this world or die and go to be with the Lord. He concluded that to depart and dwell with Christ was better by far. He decided that he was called to remain for the time, however, since that was better for his fellow believers (Philippians 1:21–26).

Indeed, the peace Mary and I have experienced in Jesus, together with this genuine hope in our future afterlife with God, gives us the fortitude to confront and overcome the various challenges we have faced and continue to encounter on the road of life.

---

[13] 1 Peter 1:3, NIV.

Regardless of the intensity of the troubles life throws our way, we understand that they are temporary in the context of eternity.

REFLECTIONS ON HOPE

Just as a huge gulf separates the life purpose established by ourselves and that established by God, so too is there a huge gulf between earthly hope for a good life and ultimate hope for a good afterlife. The latter is determined solely by God and found only through a relationship with Jesus Christ.

According to the apostle Peter, faith in Jesus produces a living hope because Jesus survived the grave and lives on forever. By contrast, all earthly hope ultimately dies, since one hundred percent of us will pass away sooner or later.

From a recent survey of Canadians regarding their views of God, the majority think he and heaven exist and, by extension, they're going to heaven. The genesis of these beliefs is unclear. Perhaps it's wish fulfillment or the natural desire for a happy ending. Many of those who say they believe in God think they're going to heaven based upon their moral uprightness and what they deem to be the demands of fairness!

Alternatively, and notwithstanding their belief in the existence of God, if it turns out he doesn't exist, many believe it will simply be lights out, or the death of consciousness, when they die.

Whether one believes they're heaven-bound or headed for lights out, neither alternative requires any action on their part other than to live a decent life. In a similar vein, many find it hard to believe there will be a judgment day when they face God, who, armed with perfect knowledge of their lives—every thought, word, and deed!—will judge them with absolute righteousness (Hebrews 9:27).

While the existence of God cannot be proved with mathematical certainty, the creation itself strongly points to the existence of a divine, all-powerful creator (Romans 1:20). Recent scientific discoveries increasingly support this God hypothesis.[14]

At the end of the day, the issue of God's existence won't be determined by our beliefs but rather what is true. And truth is that which corresponds to reality.

According to the Christian worldview, the ultimate reality is God—and since he is Spirit, the act of connecting with him is spiritual in nature. The system of navigation that helps us find our way to heaven is the revelation found in the Bible, enlightened by God's indwelling Holy Spirit, since the Bible declares itself to be the inspired word of God (2 Timothy 3:16). Heaven cannot be reached based upon our opinions of right and wrong or logical reasoning.

By analogy, the GPS in our cars uses algorithms to determine the optimal route between two locations, assuming no change in present traffic conditions. Since the GPS can't bridge the gap between the known and the unknown—for example, new accidents that occur en route—we must either accept this risk or mitigate it by allowing extra time for the journey.

Like the GPS, our cognitive faculties can be useful in assessing facts, such as the historical evidence supporting the Christian worldview. However, a nonbeliever can't bridge the spiritual gap between themselves and God; it can be bridged only by accepting

---

[14] Stephen C. Meyer, *The Return of the God Hypothesis* (Toronto, ON: Harper Collins, 2021).

> **Out of love, God doesn't force himself on us but has granted us the freedom to choose: we can either be lords of our own lives or make him the Lord of our lives.**

God's gracious forgiveness of our many rebellious acts (Ephesians 2:8–9).

Out of love, God doesn't force himself on us but has granted us the freedom to choose: we can either be lords of our own lives or make him the Lord of our lives. In the words of writer and teacher Dale Carnegie, "Destiny is not a matter of chance. It is a matter of choice."[15]

MARY ADDS

Now faith is the substance of things hoped for,
the evidence of things not seen.[16]
—Author of Hebrews

In general usage, the word hope implies wishful thinking, optimism about a good outcome, or both. I have used this word far too often when trying to encourage others or demonstrate empathy when they're going through a difficult situation.

The following are some typical examples.

- I hope you feel better soon.
- I hope you have a wonderful vacation.
- I hope you have a safe flight.

---

[15] *The Art of Public Speaking,* Dale Carnegie (New York, NY: Skyhorse Publishing, 2018), location 309.

[16] Hebrews 11:1, NKJV.

- I hope you have exceptional success in your new business venture.

None of these statements carries genuine substance. Even when heartfelt, they are at best kind sentiments or warm wishes. Sometimes we use the word hope to be as encouraging as possible even when we actually feel quite uncertain about the outcome. Other times we're simply trying to be polite. As a Canadian, I'm inclined to be polite!

Per the foregoing scripture, biblical hope has substance to back it up. It's animated by my faith in God, which rests firmly on the truth of his word as recorded in the Bible. My hope in him is grounded in his demonstrated faithfulness over the course of my life so far and his many wonderful promises for the life to come. While I may waver in the face of life's inevitable challenges, I always have hope based upon God's word and the many times he has whispered comforting assurances to my heart.

WAKE-UP CALL

Do you know where you're going when, not if, you die? Is your hope anchored in reality? Based upon the Bible, Jesus is the ultimate reality and he offers you eternal life in his presence. We encourage you to take a risk and ask him to take charge of your life. From our experience and that of believers over the centuries, you won't regret that decision!

Conclusion

FULFILLED LIVING IS YOURS FOR THE ASKING

> I am the door. If anyone enters
> by me, he will be saved and
> will go in and out and find
> pasture. The thief comes only
> to steal and kill and destroy. I
> came that they may have life
> and have it abundantly.[17]
>
> —Jesus

MARY AND I have discovered that Jesus is the doorway, the portal, to experiencing life filled with purpose, peace, and hope. Accepting him as Lord and Savior is the key to discovering why we exist in the first place (our purpose) and then fulfilling that purpose. By living out our God-given purpose, we move from our old state of chasing after but never really realizing a satisfying life to a new state of fulfilled living found only in a personal relationship with God.

As a result of our decision to turn our lives over to Jesus, we were able to tap into the peace of God regardless of what the world threw at us. Moreover, we have been able to face every situation, no matter how challenging, knowing that our ultimate hope of everlasting life is absolutely secure in the presence of our wonderful creator. That hope is anchored in Jesus's promise of reconciliation with our heavenly Father, per his words in the book of John: *"I am*

---

[17] John 10:9–10, ESV.

the way and the truth and the life. No one comes to the Father except through me" (John 14:6, NIV).

Knowing our purpose in and of itself doesn't produce fulfillment without purpose-driven action. In the same manner, knowing that abundant life is accessible through Jesus Christ accomplishes nothing unless we take action by accepting his offer of forgiveness. In his infinite wisdom, God didn't create human robots. Rather, he honored our image-bearing status by granting us the freedom to accept his offer of salvation by grace through faith (Ephesians 2:8–9).

We encourage you to take the next step and ask God to take charge of your life. For information on how you can do just that, please turn to the appendix.

Appendix

KNOWING GOD PERSONALLY

THE FOLLOWING POINTS explain God's purpose in creating you, the obstacle standing in the way of your fulfilling his purpose, God's solution to your problem, and your response to his solution. Taken together, they are the pathway to a personal relationship with God. All four points are based upon the Bible.

GOD'S LOVE

God loves you and created you to know him personally. He offers a wonderful plan for your life. The Bible speaks of his love:

> For God so loved the world, that he gave his only Son, that whoever believes in him should not perish but have eternal life. (John 3:16)

And his plan:

> And this is eternal life, that they know you, the only true God, and Jesus Christ whom you have sent. (John 17:3)

This is wonderful news, but there's an obstacle standing in the way of our entering into a personal relationship with God.

OUR CONDITION

Because we are sinful and separated from God, we cannot know him personally or experience his love and plan.

People are sinful:

> ...for all have sinned and fall short of the glory of
> God... (Romans 3:23)

WHAT IS SIN?

In his love for us, God granted us free will rather than programming us to make choices in conformity with his plans and purposes. Because we chose to go our own way without regard to God, our relationship with him was broken. This self-will and our choosing to satisfy our own desires independent of God is evidence of what the Bible calls sin.

We demonstrate this attitude by being selfish, openly disobeying God's will as revealed in the Bible, or by simply ignoring him.

People are separated from God:

> For the wages of sin is death, but the free gift
> of God is eternal life in Christ Jesus our Lord.
> (Romans 6:23)

Many people try to connect with God and establish a personal relationship with him through their own efforts. These include living good lives or adhering to religious activities they think will satisfy God.

However, we inevitably fail because no one can live up to God's standard of righteousness. While it would seem our situation is hopeless, God himself provides the bridge over which we can cross into a relationship with him.

GOD'S RESPONSE

Jesus Christ is God's only provision for our sin. Through him alone we can know God personally and experience his love and plan.

He died in our place:

> ...but God shows his love for us in that while we
> were still sinners, Christ died for us. (Romans 5:8)

He rose from the dead, so we may know

> that Christ died for our sins... that he was bur-
> ied, that he was raised on the third day in accor-
> dance with the Scriptures, and that he appeared
> to Cephas [Peter], then to the twelve. Then he
> appeared to more than five hundred... (1 Corin-
> thians 15:3–6)

He is the only way to God:

> Jesus said to him, "I am the way, and the truth,
> and the life. No one comes to the Father except
> through me." (John 14:6)

Jesus's sacrificial death on the cross is the bridge God created for us to have a relationship with him. By dying in our place, Jesus paid the penalty for our sins and thereby created the way for us to enter into a personal relationship with God.

In ways we cannot accomplish or even imagine, Jesus Christ provides the means by which our sins are forgiven, thus achieving reconciliation with God.

However, simply knowing the foregoing three points—God's plan, our problem, and God's solution—in itself doesn't achieve reconciliation with God.

OUR RESPONSE

We must individually receive Jesus Christ as Savior and Lord. Then we can know God personally and experience his love and plan.

We must receive Jesus Christ:

> But to all who did receive him, who believed in his name, he gave the right to become children of God... (John 1:12)

We receive Jesus through faith:

> For by grace you have been saved through faith. And this is not your own doing; it is the gift of God, not a result of works, so that no one may boast. (Ephesians 2:8–9)

Reconciliation with God is his free gift to us, one which we receive by faith in him. It can't be achieved by our own efforts, since none of them can possibly bridge the enormous gap between us and the perfectly righteous God.

By receiving and putting our trust in Jesus, we cross this chasm, thereby entering into a relationship with God and experiencing his abundant life.

We receive Jesus Christ by personal invitation:

> Behold, I stand at the door and knock. If anyone hears my voice and opens the door, I will come in to him and eat with him, and he with me. (Revelation 3:20)

Receiving Jesus Christ involves turning away from the self and toward God (repentance) and trusting Jesus to forgive our sins, come into our lives, and make us what he wants us to be. As recorded in John 3, this is what Jesus meant when he told the religious leader that he must be "born again" to be made right with God. In essence, when we receive and trust in Jesus, we enter into a wholly new life (2 Corinthians 5:17).

Agreeing intellectually with these points or having an emotional experience isn't enough. We receive Jesus Christ by faith as an act of our will and from the heart. Flowing from this decision, we put Jesus rather than self at the center of our lives.

PRAYER

God knows your heart. He isn't so concerned with your precise words but rather the attitude of your heart. The following is a suggested prayer you can speak to God:

> Lord Jesus, I want to know you personally. I'm sorry for disregarding you and living my own way without seeking your will for me. Thank you for dying on the cross for my sins and granting me eternal life. I turn from my own ways and open the door to your ways. Please be my Savior and Lord. Be in charge of my life and enable me to know and follow your lead. Make me the kind of person you want me to be.

ASSURANCE

When you receive Jesus, you can rest in the assurance that he isn't only your Savior but also your friend. Know that your life is totally secure in him.

The Bible promises eternal life to all who receive Jesus Christ:

> And this is the testimony, that God gave us eternal life, and this life is in his Son. Whoever has the Son has life; whoever does not have the Son of God does not have life. I write these things to you who believe in the name of the Son of God, that you may know that you have eternal life. (1 John 5:11–13)

Thank God often that Jesus Christ is in your life and will never leave you (Hebrews 13:5). You can know this truth based upon his promise that Jesus Christ lives in you and you have eternal life from the very moment you invite him in.

ABOUT THE AUTHORS

OVER THE COURSE of his business career, Garth Jestley has held many senior leadership positions in the financial services industry and, for many years, served as CEO of an international investment management firm.

Subsequently, Garth assumed the role of executive director of LeaderImpact, the mission of which is to help marketplace leaders across Canada and in dozens of other countries explore the relevance of faith in God in their professional and personal lives.

Garth and Mary came to faith as adults after separate life-changing encounters with Jesus. They are leaders in their local church and have long ministered together in various teaching capacities, including participating in their church's International Leaders School of Ministry in various countries around the world.

ALSO BY GARTH JESTLEY

More Than Your Business Card:

A Wake-up Call for Leaders Desiring to Follow
Jesus in the Marketplace.
9781957616100

Many of us, if we're honest, leave God at home when we go to work because we don't feel comfortable sharing our faith in the secular marketplace. But what if God has called you to business? This book confirms business leadership as a legitimate, important, and deeply fulfilling way to follow Jesus. It provides practical guidance for stepping into your calling as Christ's ambassador while simultaneously fulfilling your mandate as a business leader.

From his encounters as a seasoned business executive, Garth Jestley believes most leaders today are essentially unaware of their need for God. In the busyness and pressures of professional life, they are constantly distracted from considering matters of ultimate importance. As their peer, you may be the only one who can reach them with the good news of Jesus.

Through exploring the realities, principles, and practices of representing Jesus in the marketplace, this book encourages Christian business leaders to wake up and respond to God's call on their work life. It will help you realize the importance of your influence within the business sphere and tap into your unique qualifications to make a sizable impact for the Kingdom of God.

"As a business veteran himself, Garth articulates the profound opportunity and humbling responsibility we have as marketplace leaders to authentically live and lead by Kingdom values."

—Donald E. Simmonds
Chairman, The Blyth Group

"Garth has unveiled a key truth we need to embrace in this one sentence: 'When we accept our call to business, we become ambassadors for God in the secular marketplace.' Deep gratitude and thanks to Garth for inspiring the mission in all of us."

—C. Esther De Wolde, CPA, GPA
Chief Executive Officer, Phantom Screens